ELEGY OF THE SEASONS
IN THE CITY WITHOUT DOMES

Poems by Claudia Manta

CORESI

Publishing House

WWW.CORESI.NET

CLAUDIA MANTA

ELEGY OF THE SEASONS
IN THE CITY WITHOUT DOMES

Poems

WWW.CORESI.NET

This book is published in print and digital editions.

Cover design: Viorica Didic Vlas
Illustrations supplied by the author.

ISBN: 9798719757421 (KDP print edition)

For more information on this book, please write to
coresi@coresi.net
For the bilingual edition of this book, please go to
http://bit.ly/ClaudiaManta

www.coresi.net
www.LibrariaCoresi.ro

Dedicated
with lots of love
to my father, journalist Dumitru Nicu

TABLE OF CONTENTS

April Rains

Under the red eaves, two birds are frozen and it rains,
Trees do not know how to blossom, April is late,
In the mantle of frozen flowers, spring has forgotten us,
With wet hair she runs, in an unreleased dance.

The sunbeams on your shoulders, you return from the hasty road,
Your coat is snowy and outdated, your smile amazed,
If I could gather all the rain in one bucket,
I would overthrow them all in the Black Sea.

I expect to catch gold in my hair, to catch wind in my dreams,
To feel the aroma of late poppies, running to you laughing,
Bring you snail shells into my scarf,
Smiles in bouquets and red eggs, in the door.

But it rains, over frowns, over thoughts,
It feels like time is weird, shaking, it's cold,
Splashed crystals hit the asphalt,
Nature is resurrected under teared eyes.

March 29, 2018

The Dancer

In the dust of the floor she was turning,
With loose curls, painted points,
Clear smile on purple lips,
In pirouettes, her silhouette melted.

And the guitar was screaming, the piano was crying,
And she was spinning in the dust of stars, my memories,
I was dancing with her, the Universe was dancing,
God was watching us.

God chose her,
Joy to share, and history and dreams,
A girl with long hair like lilac blossom, eyes like the lake,
In which sparkle lights and shadows and rainbows.

When her body is arched,
Time stops, the rhythm of the music twists,
And she dances, turns, snaps,
In the floor dust, relieving my heart.

Dancing, dancing, until noon,
When the sun disappears into cool coats,
The soul burns, the heart sings,
God listens to us.

July 6, 2017

I Love the Light of Sunset in the City

I love the light of sunset in the city,
The gentle touch of the wind,
The splash of my memories,
The ticking of the clock tower,
The abrupt rhythm of our passing life,
We do not hear it and do not feel it until tomorrow.

Tomorrow we remember yesterday or a fantasy,
Or an infallible gesture or a hope,
Made from our passion or a whisper,
Divine and young, under the stars ...

I love the sunset in the city,
A diamond on the roofs,
Rays in your blue, restless lashes,
What are you thinking about?
I was walking around the city ... Myself and God.

September 26, 2019

I Miss You, Bucharest

I miss you, Bucharest, I miss that air of the moon, in the evening
Your stoney and chipped streets by our steps,
And Jesus more beautiful in your icons,
Locked into small churches which stream the sun.

I miss bells, children with eyes of darkness,
Those old sunsets over brown roofs,
The loneliness of Dambovita river, waiving,
And the rhythm of your decadent heart, in love.

I miss you, Bucharest, the city of a lost youth,
Contained with many passions and dreams,
I find you delighted,
Like a lover who waited so long.

I miss you, Bucharest, the city of ephemeral dreams.

November 27, 2019

Love from the Stars

In the darkness of the streets, only a cigarette burns,
Tonight I tell you that I have a chest full of stars,
And my heart swollen with this love coming from above,
When the sky snows ephemeral silk laces.

All wounds are healed, when we laugh and haunt
the streets at night,
When we hold hands in a fugitive prayer,
A sign of eternity in a simple moment.

Better keep quiet, words dissolve slowly,
What to say more beautiful than an angel hug,
More than this madness touched by Heaven,
In the fall we will not forget
Ever...

This Love is coming from stars....

November 17, 2019

November Covered in Snow

November covered by snow is shaking with tears,
But you exist now and the sky seems higher, lunatic,
The sky, in love with a single star, sings,
All our stories end with a fiery embrace.

It Snows in the soul but it snows with dreams,
The wings of a thousand angels cover my sad sorrows,
The torment has since melted, of course,
You're waiting for me in the park, on a bench ... And it's snowing.

It's too early for a final love,
But there is the chance of unimaginable beauty,
Of a winter as in the stories of the grandmother,
Told in the fragrant evenings with fir tree smell.

There is a chance of endless love,
An endless string of illusions and realities,
November is the best time of year,
And yet some rebel leaves remained on the branch.

November 13, 2019

October Hopes

And our laughter was rolling in crystals, when the night's eye closed
the day,
October glittering and glowing reminds us, together,
Musk perfume and lilac flowers,
And this sunset fire, the sublime fall.

I feel like I'm born again, I feel like we're reborn,
Hand in hand under the dreams, under the open sky, who hears,
A hot and innocent prayer, mature, persistent,
An amalgam of burning hopes and desires.

And last day of fall ended, with the red sunset, vibrating,
Our hands frozen, clenched, under infinity,
And if it snows, we'll still be laughing,
And if we cry tomorrow, we will be together.

October 21, 2019

September Light

And remember the sea, bright volcanic eyes,
September among wheat fields, among sweet grapes,
Sun rings around me dancing,
Smells of corn and dried smell of woods.

The light of the early sunset, suspended between dream and reverie,
That cold, cold air, warmed by your lips, whispering the sea,
The day still lies in the sun, mimicking the summer,
Lost long ago, in the color of twilight.

And the smoky smell, of chained leaves,
White horses among the deserts, smeared with shadows of fire,
Wild manes, my cheek is crying in them,
The September light puts my soul in chains.

I live a sweet exile of dreams and deeds,
Just the thought runs like the gentle, shaky wind,
Over all my memories, young September, infatuated,
With that light of twilight, of golden fields and unlimited sky.

September 12, 2019

Snowy Roses

Snowy roses in your hand, this frozen day,
I dream of spring illusions, and the sun in my hair,
The birds are scorched with snowflakes in their wings,
Hunchbacked, the passers-by disappear.

It's a long winter, it's not like home,
The days seem nights and nights dark holes,
We count the moments that seem eternal,
We count the lighted, smoked lanterns.

Your white and soft hands loosen my curls,
You smell like the forest and the snow flowers of the sky,
I'm trying to twist my hopes,
And abandon myself in your will...

But this tumult of dreams, this snow that haunts my soul,
I can barely breathe in the night, whispering prayers that burn
And this winter is an inferno,
A quilt with unfinished stories about a country on another land.

Snowy roses in your hand, this frozen day,
I kiss cold petals, memories of forgotten childhood,
It's snowing and you warm up your hands smiling,
You smell of spring and field flowers.

January 29, 2018

End of August

Gentle August, old pendulum, polished with illusions,
It beats us on the eyelashes, with dew and butterflies,
Crickets greased with passions, vivid and desperate,
They play a symphony of notes under the window.

In shades of blue, we walk on the infernal streets,
Sprinkled with summer memories, you and I, hurry steps,
Gold sandals with high heels, crosswalks,
In order to gather as many solar images, in August.

And it's that nostalgia, that hard feeling to say,
That we feel now, in late August,
One moment children, one moment adults, with lessons ready,
Feel or grasp, a beginning steeped in desire.

And August is gentle, when I cry you shake, amazed,
You try to lift my chin, I tremble, crying inconsolable,
It's the most thrilling month of the year, August at the end,
With crickets and butterflies, and the illusions of the ravaged
summer.

August 26, 2019

Saint Elijah

Saint Elijah with cloudbeard, blue thunder eyes,
In the sky, he throws sparks, shakes the stars,
You once brought me gladioli, what thrilling flowers,
Cried with your tears, sprinkled with shades of red and yellow....

Today, the years of the time seem dreams, the years of youth,
I live an exile of thoughts, polished with the gold of lonely sunsets,
And yet time triumphs, makes promises to me,
About youth without old age and life without death.

Who am I supposed to believe? How did I fall into this trap?
When I feel like I'm a child, even though I have silver hair strands,
On my shoulders the sun was still kissing me, with passion,
It was Saint Elijah when you brought me gladioli and tears.

July 20, 2019

Just the Moment

Me, without feeling the sea on my body, in crystals,
Solar hugs and breeze in ribbons, on eyelashes,
I wouldn't live here, I wouldn't breathe youth.

And life is a intertwining of facts and dreams,
A pile of hope, scattered disappointments,
Just the moment is star, just the moment is power,
The nectar from which I sip my rebellious joy.

I'm waiting for you to call me, on the rocky shore,
Reddened in the sunset of July, on fire,
And the steps to run among algae,
Only the moment knows us, just the moment lifts us.

July 14, 2019

Summer Rain

Summer rain, comes and goes, my heart is bitter,
Beauty triumphs, a corner of heaven lost with blue eyelashes,
charmed,
Song of birds spoiled and losts on roofs.

Summer rain, I cry and you cry, you shield your rebellious thoughts,
Desert of austere words and nonsense,
I better stop and look at the stars, the garden of saints, perfumed
with myrrh and hope.

Summer rain, after your flood of sun, burn the strands of my stories,
unwritten,
Vainly spoken in thought, told,
Without you summer is a hell of longing,
A deserted heaven of nobless.

July 13, 2019

Midsummer Day

Midsummer day, with poppies blown away by the wind, kissed by
fairy tales virgins,
Through the rain of flowers, I am dancing for you,
Wrapped hand in hand, we turn into the rings ...
It is raining with rebellious fluff and fragrance, of lilies and star
flowers,
In the hot sun, my heart burns, in the shadow, is the ice of my
torments,
It's the sky above all, the mirror of a desired lake in azure.
I'm afraid to cry for such beauty,
And in this balsamic air, angels touch my hair,
Father s kisses, on golden curls, rebellious.
Midsummer day, illusory game of fairy tales virgins, secret wishes,
And flowers on braided locks, aster kisses,
Symphonies of forests and celestial dreams ...

June 24, 2019

May Morning

Hey, morning full of sun, your eyes full of color, Spring,
Paint with azure and cheeks with cherry blossoms and raspberries,
I stretch out my bare arms, in a frantic embrace,
In the air fragrant and powdery with aromas of flower.

May only blossomed in one evening,
When I was sitting and watching on the terrace, the sky overflowed
                                        with stars,
Braided on the shawl on my frozen, desperate shoulders,
Under your touch, when you whispered: spring is coming!

On the glossy asphalt my steps are measured, with a slight trot,
                                        without a care,
When the wind smashes my soaked scarf with perfume of iris and
                                        butterfly,
May intimidated by the nonchalance of your words,
Plated with the sun of my expectations, ordinary ...

May 6, 2019

May Cries

Waiting is a hope detached from the dream,
When May cries and your silence is an abyss,
Spring flakes kiss us thrilled,
I hear angels knocking on windows, frozen.

Maybe it's not the angels, it's just my thoughts,
Or the magnolias melted after the rain of stars,
Maybe silence is an answer to my questions,
It's May and I don't see a single petal on your eyelashes.

Who stole the spring, the sleeked girl,
With rich locks, willow eyes in painted green,
Maybe you stopped her from coming, running,
Maybe it stopped somewhere between heaven and earth.

Maybe May cries and waits for a word...

May 2, 2019

A Young Spring

A young and clear spring, through the frozen city,
Love is the sign placed on the walls, in the renovated district,
Hand in hand, crushing time, I forgot to catch your eyes, your
doubts ...

The lamps tremble, the flakes melt flying,
The sky rebukes me, it is hunted and woven, like a young horse,
painted,
On the web of infinity, where I dive with you, in my thoughts.

Love is the sign on the walls and in the windows,
Not to forget that every moment is sublime and we, hold hands,
Through the district full of color and sun and frozen wind, flavored
with spring scents ...

March 17, 2019

I Want

I want to cling to a hope, like to a cradle from the horizon,
To savoir my moments in the summer wind, With hair rolled in fire,
And like a child detached from fairy tales, palms open upwards,
To the sky cleared by stars, and dripped with prayers.

I want to have a little chance, towards you and a fugitive dream,
To run to the place that gathers the sea in the maze,
And with the love of yesterday, on the reddened shore of the sunset,
Let's pick stars and lovers whispers.

And the shells are singing the story of the oceans in the dream,
Of the waves breaking, when I come towards you, flying, in the
clouds,
I want to get my chance again,
Like you are waiting, smiling, floating ....

January 4, 2019

When I Am with You

When I'm with you, I have everything, and without you I have
nothing,
I conquered the earth with love and I have no regrets, no matter
how tiny,
Hand and hand on a narrow bridge, on a boiling sea,
We sail, under the stars and under their sifted paints.

Sifted with illusions, lies, the mirror of the ugly world,
But who cares, your smile is smooth, the warmth of your shoulders
bewilders me,
When it s snowing, I am not cold, petals flow from your words of
love.

And I'm not afraid, isn t fear a deserted universe?
When I am with you, the days are white, sunny,
And it snows with the warm fluff of angels,
From the Heaven covered with God.

February 4, 2019

The Hope

The day is still gray in the frozen city,
And the snow moves from the decorated sky,
With an angel's tear and a cherub's cloud,
And in my heart a hope grows, like a delirium.

I think of You again, a look without a word,
Eyes that are drawn to me from an unmatched Heaven,
And the hope comes to me like a melting March,
Which in the daylight, grace drips on my forehead.

God is not only in the altars, He is moving incandescently,
Over our thoughts, over deeds and mistakes,
And I also understood that He would appear anytime,
Even in the house with ghosts, when I'm alone, crying.

He will also appear starved on a street,
With a white, outstretched hand, and his hair unrolled,
He will appear in the smile of a baby with jade eyes,
Or in the heartless sigh of a banal passer-by.

And the hope grows high, like the clouds that rise,
To understand the horizon, gray, incomprehensible,
I have never lived so much winter even when I was a kid,
But I find you, love, in this divine turmoil.

January 15, 2019

In the End

And finally it is you with your white, cryptic fingers,
Weaving images from the abyss, as only you know,
Tearing down the tears that gathered like a mountain lake,
As cold and bitter, under the blooming sky.

And finally it is you, with your unrolled locks,
Falling a little on your shoulders, burdened by questions,
Autumn illusions,
And every whisper you sing gives birth to stars.

And finally it is you, with your blue eyes,
Elongated by perl eyelids and pure,
You sing to me symphonies from the petals,
And you create so many stories, captivated by your dreams.

And finally it is you, my last lucky star,
On a planet with a blunt face, fear, loneliness,
One last great gesture, one last chance,
Towards life ...

January 22, 2019

I Promise You

Let's remember the summer, the acacia forest shivering in secret,
That fire of sunset, trembling on the lake,
Hair twisted by the wind and twisted in romance,
Gray night' s eye puzzling the stars.

Let's remember the love in colorful scarves,
Crystalline laughter in majestic accords,
The perfume dripped on the white arms,
With which we caress the linden trees, scattered by nights.

And I promise you that winter will be over,
And we will hold hands again, picking up blue flowers,
With the waves on our ankles, like snakes,
And the golden sun dripped from all our dreams.

I promise you...

December 21, 2018

This City

December came with sunshine, little sparrows on empty roofs,
Cold, damp air, aromas of cinnamon, myrrh and fir in celebration,
And I run with my cheeks burning, to grab your hand again,
To walk slowly through the decorated city, warmed up and
illuminated.

Labyrinths of color, smoke from the furnaces, noise,
I load with this momentum that belongs to the eternal sidewalks,
Eyes of hasty passers-by, a smile in one go,
And I pray to my saints to bring me comfort.

The comfort of lost longing, for a country far away,
What I left once, when I had a heavy heart,
In the meantime, that pain has transformed into stars,
In a dream I'm missing, with fairy tales domes.

But I also love this city, his aristocratic air,
Old red houses, tired lanterns,
The tower that reaches the sky, lost and austere,
And your great love, as a protective whisperer,

... whispers in my ear, I love you endlessly ...

December 4, 2018

Winter is Coming

The naked, empty trees sing the autumn symphony,
Tomorrow the furious winter stops among us.
Slender, white and frozen, with maddening locks,
Loose angel loops and silver shoes.

Purple smile on the lips out of the powder on the snow,
And with eyes shining like the moon, trembling in a cloak,
White, fine, like light, on an endless Sky,
I'm waiting for you to come, love, to a station, without rhythm.

And the city sifts dreams, transformed and full of night,
Wasted by the winter wind, the tears on the fir trees,
If I could ever forget that he left summer behind,
Her solar joy, the ethereal joy.

You draw angels on asphalt, from a thousand stories,
We look silently at the moon, gathering fading clouds,
And the memory haunts us—of the days we loved each other
And forgot that time passes, so rough, aged.

November 29, 2018

Winter Evening

Snow ghosts on the windows, I close my eyes,
Butterflies kisses on my lips,
I'm still burning my mind,
The pendulum rings the time of the night, secular,
And dreams come to light with the smell of fir.

There was nothing left of summer, scarf of flowers, broken into
thrills,
On my shoulders, shaking with sighs,
Of a deep longing, of the sea and the sun,
Fairy tales, told in taverns, illuminated by stars.

Through the snow fast steps, hurried steam,
Your warm hand, and a whispered song,
You picked all the snowflakes in your hair,
Every snowy winter haunts my heart.

November 17, 2018

The City without Domes

The city without domes enjoys softly the autumn leaves,
The rebellious rusty fall from the old trees,
I told all the stories and I embedded all the poems,
Wonderful summer memories from scattered places.

I was left with only the open sky, the largest dome of the world,
Under the blushing clouds I pray and cry, I am speechless,
Beggars bounce among cards, do not ask for more than a coin,
Falling in their goddess palm.

I still have to see in their blue eyes a part of You,
To know that a piece of a broken icon is holy,
With my tight hand running to the coming train,
But far, I can not run away from the town without domes.

But You are here and you are anywhere,
With blond hair, prolonged, and tears,
Who can see you, when you are light as the flake and full of ashes,
Jesus of our heart, in the city without domes.

September 27, 2018

Promises for July

It's the wind that blows my memories, soft and tender, the smell of
pine,
And that grandfather's look in the door, in your house, is waiting for
me soon,
Bouquet of hopes in the white hydrangeas, mature trees with laurel
leaves,
When summer whispers solar promises and a lot of green blended
with steam.

And you promise me it's a long summer and her coat is unfolded into
frills,
Over the love between us and over the flights of cranes,
And I'm laughing and thinking that time stops, a drop of luck,
In my palm, in my heart twitching, so young and so tall.

And you promise me we will both be in the clouds,
To our parallel world, bathed in myrrh and in the foreheads of saints,
Which I kiss so hard, it is July, and it smells like flower,
Like sun-drenched buildings, under your eyes, with teared eyelashes.
It is still summer and much more until I will cry of fear,
That frost catches on us a gust of wind and rain,
You promised me that summer would be long and we would be
holding hands, under the pines,
That we will fly over Aegean sea like pigeons over the stars.

July 18, 2018

I Wish Summer Never Ended

I wish summer never ended,
In a torrid noon like I am flying in the clouds,
Joy encompasses my being, a woven shawl of flowers,
From roses and chestnuts and golden dreams.

We ran hand in hand after an illusion,
We have stumble in so much rigidity,
When life is simple, a fragile kiss,
Your smell of cologne and the embrace of the stars in the evening.

I wish the summer did not end, the lullabies of the sunsets,
And my fire hair, caught in a loop,
Under your arm, under the blue, acacia shower.

July 2, 2018

The Lake

The lake brings us eternal memories, its sacred image,
Green and blue of the algae, waves on our ankles,
Chestnut flowers carved carpets, over dreams,
The coast of a fairy tale, sandy and withered.

I'm walking on the pontoon with light steps, jerky,
Your hand is warm and you followed me,
A guitar complains about the story, vibrant,
A young man smokes steam, with his hair like coals.

And the wind is destroying the tainted trees,
It is whispering on my lips muffled sights,
I hear the children running without a care, on the sea.

The lake is struggling under the mantle of the sky,
It's like my heart, the poetry of a dwarf city,
With lavender smell and tangled accords.

The lovers tell gentle words, under the willow trees,
Your eyes are full of tears and you are bare feet,
The last star kisses me on my temples.

July 9, 2018

How Beautiful Summer Is

How beautiful summer is! The youth of nature, a bright childhood,
Chestnut Symphony and Blue Glory,
The rhythmic dance of the green leaves, and your green eyes,
Overtaken by untold tears, ancient thoughts.

Afternoons are hot and it smells of fire and sun,
Pigeons are cooing, they invent a majestic fly,
Over all these red and obsolete roofs,
It's my memories, all my moods.

Arms in arms two old ladies are swinging, basil in their fragile hands,
The brides have scrolled their veils, the heat is torching the kiss,
I walk in white on streets full of creeps,
The wind caresses me, it brings me flowers.

What a beautiful summer! Young girl with beads made of pansies,
The golden ribbons of her hair, the illusions of the sun,
You are waiting for me on a terrace your elbow leaning against the bar,
Your tan smile stirs me again.

What a beautiful summer! Standing on a laced bench,
My whirling hair pounds slightly on my back,
It smells of lime and grass,
Acacia flowers falls slowly on our eyelids.

June 28, 2018

June throughout the City

June and us through the city, on the glistening cobblestones, we slide,
Here is a flower; here is a pot, a little shop,
The wind blows from behind and takes us easily to the lake,
The sky is bent and hunted, the trees have jade manes.

I'm ravished by scents, flags moving and drops fall on our face,
I'm sticking to you, you're wearing the cane umbrella,
Here is a silk boutique, here is a kiosk with memories,
June through city, my chest is full of wind and acacia fragrance.

We lose ourselves chuckling on the streets in colorful rainbows,
It's raining, it's sunny, it's the sky deep or like a big wave,
Under the trees there were traces of flower, falling
In my hair, on your lashes.

June and us through the city, strolling, no care in the world,
Here is a deserted terrace, here is a solitary lace bench,
You picked for me all the acacia flowers, you keep them in your arms,
White and eternal and painted with sun.

June 4, 2018

Flowers and Streetcars

Hot fire lines under my feet,
I hear the rumbling and the smell of wroth iron,
My hair is blowing in a wind from nowhere,
It came from the heavens, and from zenith.

It's the town weathered with petals, lilac and blooms,
The petunias are in thin summer dresses,
In purple and in pink and in yellow, solar,
I'm playing with a lilac flower, fragranced.

And with the window open I breathe without ceasing,
The smell of green and nature in bloom,
On the hot, shining lines,
The streetcar runs, the street as a legend appears, disappears...

And at one end you are waiting, so tall and astonishing,
Where were you? You have a flower in your hand,
Hidden under your thin, summery coat,
You put it in my hair, shy and hesitant.

Hot fire lines beneath my feet,
I crossed a whole city to see you,
We climb back, by chance, into the same streetcar,
My hair is blowing in the wind, your flower is gone.

May 24, 2018

Summers without You

What are summers without you?
What are the pines without the perfume of the sea nearby?
When I called you, a star fell,
And your little steps have melted the shores.

What are summers without you?
Pigeons without angel wings?
You are for me the scent of eternity,
You are my sure gate to God.

What are summers without you?
Lace scarves without the sun shining shoulders?
And the tears I cried all of them,
Holding the image of your fragrant body in my arms?

What are the summers without you, Father?
Simple abysses without memories,
Days without sun and azure,
And endless love poured into bitter cups.

What are summers without you?
Always hoping and always dreaming,
In the harbor the blue ship whistled,
And you were there, in the eternal summer of my young age,
I'll be with you again, wait for me, I will come!

October 24, 2017

Autumn Thoughts

I caught a thread of the fall in my hair, and I danced,
With my arms open like a forgotten albatross,
Dancing, I fell in love with you ...
When your steps come closer to mine, with no words spoken.

And I danced, defying the fall,
Which, on the window, cried with mums in her arms,
Shivering and wailing, with her unblinking eyes,
When your hand on my waist turned, I was falling for you ...

And so they go summers and dreams, always dancing, always in love,
Here it comes the fall in a rusty cloak, the same standard.
The same rhythm, the same shouted to God,
The answer is a whisper: I have not forgotten you!

October 12, 2017

Poem for a Friend

Let's talk on the terrace, in the evenings, listening to the rhythm of
the falling stars,
You leaning against the lavender pot, and a lazy smoking incense,
Running the long line of forgotten memories, silk of the moon in my
hair,
And poems crying from a book left on the blue and old divan.

And you put pearls on a fine thread, broken, the cat is playing with
the thread,
With the eyes of the feline, the whiskas full of light,
Was it yesterday when we were in the orchard? You sip a coffee and
smile at me,
The clock has mastered the hours, the moments, I lost myself in
stories.

As two children holding their hands, like the tears that come,
Years have gone leaving mad traces or cold memories,
But I like to laugh and cry around you, a fluid sentiment,
A friend goes, another comes, but you are a constant universe.

June 21, 2018

In My Stellar City

I cried to you in my dream, and you did not hear me,
And I walk on the street lost by memories, blurred,
In a city of stellar name and fame,
But who cares about all this, who is throbbing?

Who cares that time has passed by and killed our youth,
Our kids drive cars and look for homes,
We fancy sipping an aromatic coffee and Irish liqueur on a terrace,
Old fashioned in our words, still followed by passions.

I cried to you in my dream, and you did not hear me,
I'm trying to cling to an unreal world for an answer to all,
Getting rid of the reality that hurts me, it's cold,
From the gray and infernal days to the lack of sun kissed domes.

And yet I love these sidewalks, the smell of Thai and bitter flavors,
I love the street with the name of "Yonge" and the history of the
                                                    past,
I will not meet a milestone a saint, I do not care,
There are so many homeless with a beard and no wealth.

And poverty is virtue and holiness, in a stellar city,
Today the breeze is sweet; the gusts cool my face,
I cried to you in my dream, and you did not hear me,
I have dried my tears waiting: I love life!

April 30, 2018

Hey, Tell Me

Hey, tell me we will laugh again,
With so much lust, so much joy,
That the rays will draw on our faces,
Marine decors.

As the curtains will be flipping,
Revealing the image of the sea,
And we will meet again on the shore,
With the soles caressed by waves, saline.

Hey, tell me, the winter won't reign forever,
Over thoughts and over dreams,
The summer will light like a lantern,
Over our retold stories.

Hey, tell me the jasmine will blossom,
Because you have the power to move stars,
That the pigeons will open their wings,
Over our endless grief.

Hey, tell me a simple word,
For you, I have crossed the skies,
I want my heart to feel joy,
And an endless love.

March 11, 2018

The Winter

The flakes fall abundantly, imitating an inflamed dance,
My cheeks burn, melt,
My memories are insane.

Faceless passers scratch the asphalt, with the snowy hats,
I'm waiting for you next to the train, with my white hands,
Strangling the snowy scarf on my chest.

It's the winter, she is tall, with a frozen smile,
Who would want to marry,
An old girl with a body that is dry?

You are waiting for me smiling,
Let's run, with a train of imagination,
Towards a dream country, from the abyss.

But the train screaming, puffing,
On windows, the angels drew,
The whispers of those who, outside, have frozen.

And in this sweet torment, however, a baby will be born,
Whose destiny will defeat worlds and wonders,
Whose rounded hands will cushion the earth.

And the flakes fall abundantly on his robe,
And his blonde lashes by a mother are kissed,
And the cold will not freeze him ever, that he is the Lord.

December 12, 2017

Valentine's Day

I am charged with the light of the city, walking on ice,
On glass flowers, solar illusions spun into streams,
My locks are sifted by dreams, in the morning,
Warm flakes fall over the ridges of blocks, steel heights.

But the sun speaks to me about the legend of summer,
From the days you laugh, I laugh and we blend with the afternoon,
I am charged with the hope of a return and illusions,
Long walks, under flowered vaults.

But this city, though frozen,
It loads me with life, I breathe it in my chest,
A little piece of every street corner, every maze of names,
You are part of it, you are part of me ...

The city of youth on Valentine's Day,
With red hearts in windows and the smell of raspberries,
Come to a terrace to blur memories,
Let's drink some green tea and cheat the winter....

February 14, 2019

The Same Linden Tree

A linden tree grew from the asphalt, with ravishing flavors,
Not its time yet, but it's green and full of candor,
Next to a deserted house, a temple without idols,
And we go holding hands, and I jump in sandals...

I remember its scent when it touched my face with its branches,
We were still holding hands, me with a light skirt, satin and petals,
I cried then, so much beauty in garbage, what a stupor,
It's another spring now and it grew greener, bigger...

And every year, holding hands, the same wonder, a shy smile, a
          fugitive look,
My hair flies, I lean on you, spoiled and solitary,
On the same obsolete boulevard, on the same street,
In that deserted corner, with the same number, 66, the linden tree
          reigns.

May 10, 2018

Oh, Mexico

Oh, Mexico, in light dresses and ruffles,
Shy and full of floral passions,
Your hair shriveled in the sun, golden at dusk,
The seagulls jump on the sand and the guitar crying in the arched
and tanned artist s hands.

Oh, Mexico, your sensual, fragrant dance, in the evening,
Salty and soft lips, and astral dreams,
Bare feet we run on the shore, in rocky rhythms,
I would live here for a lifetime, listening to your rhythm sung by the
waves ...

March 9, 2019

A Strange Face

In the speed of the train wheels, a foreign face, smiling, dreaming,
In front of me, leaf symphony, inflamed October,
Your story, mine, our story,
Interspersed images on the weeping window.

And my hand on the warm velvet, the empty bench,
A vague whimper of wheels and tender swaying,
You in my mind and heart beating like a poplar,
In the chase of the train wheels, deafening.

And give me a piece of paper to write a note at random,
I let it fly in the wind, with my thoughts,
When your figure disappears, a coat fluttering, a foreign face, a dart
                                        in heart...

October 16, 2018

Downtown

And I go, hurriedly, with my eyes up, in the sky of an unfinished block,
Or my eyes on the asphalt, where the pigeons turn in circles,
                                        chattering, savoring,
Pieces of dry bread, thrown by a homeless with beard,
Blue eyes full of fog.

And a lady shakes her vaporous umbrella,
And a gentleman lights a cigarette which makes me sick,
And I'm going hurrying, jumping, thinking what I'll meet in my
                                        journey,
Maybe a figure known and full of life.

Sirens, lights and Swarovski crystals,
So many red flowers and humongous buildings,
And I miss memorial houses with brick and columns,
With dusty inscriptions and stairs of shabby wood.

I miss the years of my youth, when everything was strange, but all
                                        plausible,
And the new world that opened to me before,
The lilac blossomed among the stones, and what a flavor,
Someone, in a hurry, struck me with a briefcase ...

And I go hurrying, striding, staring at the sky, or eyes on the asphalt,
A Saint might live in this city?
The wind blows with the aroma of coffee,
And among the rays of sunshine and passers-by, I feel like in a Heaven
                                        on earth.

June 6, 2017

How Many Nights

How many nights do I spend in tears, your memory calling?

And the dome stars over the deep, silver sea,
Lights extinguished on the hill of your greatness, and you were
silent,
Together with eternity and infinite Heaven.

When you have everything and you feel that you have nothing, that
you are a shadow in infinity,
When you go abroad in a beautiful, secluded city,
Then your solar expression, your ecstatic flower fragrance,

It comes back like an angel with wings of light, in my charged soul.

Jesus in the Mall

Glitter, perfume, strong essences, a fragile manechin arm,
A summer dress, in a stained glass window,
And bursting music, kids, grandparents, parents,
And young people of a charming beauty … at the mall!

And I walk softly, with my thoughts all over the place,
And overwhelmed by a special longing, a gloomy state of ignorance,
Or nonsense, with perfume-soaked noses and narrowed eyes,
From a total misunderstanding of my declining state.

And all of a sudden, that tall figure, in a white robe, blue skies,
Hair like a wheat field chain, a warm smile, and translucent eyes,
A hot wave, like the sea, a joy without form and equal, a heart raised
in another,
And I laugh and cry, because He is with me in the mall!

And I don't walk anymore, I walk on the water, and the world is
detached from ideas,
For He with me, and I with Him, fear no more,
In the maze of unanswered questions, he answered,
Smile almost extinguished on holy lips, smell of cypress, and a look
of zenith.

Jesus in the mall came …

October 10, 2019

On the Shore

On the shore, we ran free and windswept, with the gold of the skies
in our hair,
On the lips the kiss of the sea salt, mixed with the nectar of the
moment,
The sweetness of a unique December,
On the rhythm of reggae and palm trees dressed in Christmas attire.

It seems eternal this moment, the universe opened in heaven,
I breath the sea, the sun and your perfume,
I close my eyes and subscribe to an absolute love.

And I am never saturated by footsteps on the wet sand, joyful,
By this endless azure, by the embrace of the great sea,
Tell me that youth has no end,
And that love conquers all.

December 20, 2019

Moon Dust

Pour moon dust on my eyelashes, in these gray nights,
To sleep illuminated by your thoughts and your smile,
The smooth length of winter and its ignorance frightens me,
When the blizzard haunts us, without a particular reason.

Now when you slip from an unknown, intense space,
I dream of incandescent joys, new paths,
And endless walks through unfamiliar places,
Where the map splits into large waterfalls and unnavigated seas.

I understood that happiness is not just a word,
When we break winter in two, when we laugh and cry without
                                        sounding absurd,
When we gather together around the gentle fire,
In which the silhouettes of our stories grow.

Pour moon dust on my pillow, in these gray nights,
Kisses of angels and hugs of cherubs,
Fall from the living icons and the promises that come,
When love triumphs in a sublime way.

January 28, 2020

The Spring of Miracles

Take me to a white shore, in a snow-covered car,
Where the clock stops, in our immortalized moments,
Tears in our eyelashes frozen, embedded,
The steering wheel is listening to the lake.

The sun is trying to fight through the clouds,
Trembling slightly in the steam of morning,
A blond, rebellious and blond child,
Smiling above our great love.

Take me to a white shore, in a snow-covered car,
February repeats the story of winter in thoughts,
We are haunted by the spring of miracles,
Blossoming from our eternal mourn.

February 4, 2020

October

October, I'm crying in your hair,
The smell of musk and dreams,
The cascade of leaves allures me,
It twists like a fire in my deserted heart.

October, your tender touch,
With kisses of ripe apples,
The gold of the days in my locks,
Tufts of memories and rebellious whispers.

October, I want our story rewinded,
The same laughter, the same renewed hopes,
With you under the sky of questionsandwonders.

October 1, 2020

Windy Evening

Windy evening, drive away my fears,
You shiver in dispair, the trees shake,
Every street corner is a road to you,
And I hug a quiver of sighs.

Evening with wind, when I leave you,
Your sad eyes pass me to the car,
And I fly with my hair bewildered and desolate, on the roads,
In the game of rebellious lights, I want to go back to you...

Evening with wind, flickering darkness, scents of fruit and swirling
kisses,
The image of your vague, autumnal smile,
We are moving towards a world without promises,
But in the rhythm of our whispers and thoughts.

September 13, 2020

Hold Me Tight

These days, when even the angels cry, you hold me tight,
People, chained in disillusionment and despair, are falling,
The shadow of the Lord is not illuminating us anymore,
The sky is quieter than ever, the stars are flowing.

Waves of fear, on deserted streets and dismay,
The songs of the youth run on the walls of the empty room,
And with tears in my eyes, trembling and whispering,
I'll tell you again, hold me tight.

Earth is a big heart, bleeding, throbbing,
On our way to the prayer, to the icon of love,
There is another chance of life, forgiving, hoping,
Hold me tight...

March 23, 2020

Far from You

Far from you, the day seems night and the night seems day,
Dark and restless thoughts, blues,
The touch of the wind falling from my forehead,
The kiss of the sun cut from my temples.

You don't see that God stopped everything in place, for us, for you?
You and I are part of the crowd, all one soul,
Shaken in the night, bathed in tears in the morning,
When there is no more sunrise and the sunset seems like a ghost.

Far from everything, we are sicker than the disease itself,
We lived virtually when we could have lived in love,
Touching your sculpted, warm hands,
Now we just dream of flying towards each other,
In a hug as big as thousand stars.

April 5, 2020

A Poem for Grandma

Your soft face, like an angel, guarded my childhood,
Hands spread through my hair and my forehead full of questions,
Your deep prayer has opened my eyes to God,
When I didn't understand anything in this world.

You shone like a light, in the dark days of weeping,
You were my connection to the past, ancestral experiences,
And I bow to your suave memory,
Your sublime smile, dear grandmother.

And now from the frame, your eyes stare at me, dearly,
You go to a world full of love,
And please, in secret, with tears covered eyelashes,
Be the angel of our sorrowful hearts.

Dear Grandma, I love you ...

April 21, 2020

Keep the Moment

Keep the moment just for me, when you will come,
Keep all the kisses, covered in tears just for me,
The sky shook, at our frozen cry, out of fear,
Keep these thoughts, for when you will come ...

Keep the sun and all the stars, for when you will come,
Painting of the universe in the palm of the Deity,
The song of love and hope, the bright light of the moon,
For when you will come.

Keep the secret of love and freedom,
All the unspoken words and all the hugs,
All sunsets handled by the arm of the young night,
Just for when you will come.

And when you come, all the stars and the moon and the sun,
The huggs and the kisses, the unspoken words,
All will submit to my heart, in love,
When will you come....

April 17, 2020

Let's Wait

Let's wait a while until nature comes back to life,
Until the jasmine intoxicates us with its pearly scent,
The rhythm of us parting away is like an autumn rain in the
                                                window,
Desert is my soul, without your whispers in my scattered hair.

Let's wait seconds, days, until together,
We will step over these images as sad memories,
Tired faces and covered by masks,
But what do we care, you and I look at each other without an end.

Waiting is a gift from Heaven,
When the days fly and melt in the lonely sunset,
I have you in the icon of our stories, forever,
I have you in the smile of the Angels at dusk.

April 30, 2020

Your Day

Your day opens the nocturnal sky,
Eternal, fragrant, announcing angel songs,
May is shy and full of thoughts,
The moon is full of love, hope, and kisses.

And from my burning heart, I wish you all the best,
I embrace your shoulders with warmth and, in a whisper,
I promise that our love will go through hours, moments,
And together we will win in the tumult of sad life.

And nothing compares with this joy,
To weave from illusions, dreams that become real,
In the loneliness of life, we have the present, hand in hand,
The future now seems like a story that exists.

And from my burning heart, I wish you all the best ...

May 7, 2020

Snowy Magnolias

Snowy magnolias in the morning, tears frozen,
There is so much wonder on your face, the world seems changed,
And nothing from the past seems real anymore,
And reality is nothing more than a ghost.

We are waiting for that day, tomorrow or the day after,
When a ray of sunshine melts the ice of the petals,
Caught in a bitter game of pain,
Let's live the moment, my love, it is the only one that exists.

And you and I look at the snowy magnolias,
So much beauty and so much imprisonment,
The sublime covered with an unimaginable plague,
But let's live the moment, my love, it is the only guarantee,
whatsover.

May 9, 2020

In the Palm of God...

When the sunset lights the sky like a medallion of fire,
I miss you, us even more, your smile detached from infinity,
Fire pits on the walls go out and light up,
Shall I come to you? Or shall I wait for you in a dream?

Let's talk and laugh as much as we can, children with enchanted
voices,
Around our happiness together,
Love heals the crazy world,
Crazy about the fear of strange events.

But don't forget that you and I and everyone else,
We sit in the palm of a God with unequaled love,
And let's hope for an enlightened reality,
The promise of the sun that tomorrow is a better day ...

It s our day together ...

May 15, 2020

Today

White swans on the lake, graceful and imposing,
Your eyes say more than words can express, springs of sun,
In my hair spilled, in my heart shrouded in wonder.

We marvel at this day, bathed in light,
At the white lilac bunches and the freedom given,
Little by little, like a drop of nectar, on bitter, separated days.

Let's postpone all tormenting thoughts until autumn,
Let's look at the lake, the silence of the God over the waters, blue,
The distance between us is a memory,
And today that memory no longer hurts.

June 9, 2020

My Love

My love, it smells of peonies and flowers,
The garden sings for you, thrilled,
In the night, fires are burning, in some places,
From the courtyards, there is a smoky smell of ripe fruit on the
embers.

And my heart leaps, like a guitar chord,
Touched by trembling, tanned fingers,
It's your crystalline voice that crosses the stars,
My love, are you asleep, maybe?

I kiss your eyelids, like a touch of fragrant wind,
Like a lake with furrowed waters, your gaze crosses me,
Beyond eternity, we are hand in hand,
My love, this is an incomparable love.

June 14, 2020

On the Terrace

On the terrace, in the evening, the lilac fragrance get us drunk,
Thousands of stars twinkle in silence, kisses on our foreheads,
And thrilled by the boundlessness of heaven and love,
We don't say another word, we breathe happiness.

This is how I would like to live, with my heart stirred with joy,
Fear is an outdated, absurd memory,
And in the cool of the night, we cover our shoulders with shawls of
                                                    kisses,
The soul with the hope of a golden morning.

On the terrace, in the evening,
We ran away from the world,
As in Noah's ark, we fit perfectly,
In the sparkling and intoxicating light of a candle,
Tomorrow is a new day and we are free!

June 17, 2020

I would Like to Live Again

I would like to live again the beginning, the kiss,
Your perfume soaked in your scattered hair, your smile,
That unparalleled joy, the sky lit by caresses and mysteries,
Roars of laughter, ephemeral.

I would like to live again the freedom, the unparalleled taste of
                                          hope,
The game of questions and answers, only assumed,
When everything seemed certain in our uncertainties,
Now everything is certain and the hopes are vague, shaken.

I would like to choose you once again, out of thousands of loves and
                                          souls met, in life,
So that we can live so much happiness,
And look at the world laughing, hand in hand,
The chain of angels in eternity.

November 29, 2020

Freedom

Freedom, the last kiss in the evening, so deep,
Our steps through the city full of stars, the night extinguished in a
thought,
My friends playing the guitar, you dancing,
All of us together, on our lips the nectar of whispered words,
laughing.

Where did they all go? Freedom is the holiest thing,
Our prayers together, divine choirs, humming,
Horses running on green meadows,
The wind of salty memories, on the golden beaches.

Children in the whirlwind of the game, blushing cheeks,
Freedom, is your price so expensive?
Your beauty burns me, your taste conquers me,
Freedom, you are the holiest thing...

May 19, 2020

An Endless Love

An endless love embraces me when next to you,
Summer seems like a miracle sprinkled with flowers and dreams,
Soft, warm kisses, memories without regrets,
Our steps in duets, sing to the rhythm of the hectic street.

On the paths of love, my heart burns in me,
After the lost youth that seems to belong to you,
But we do not miss on the moment, it is destined for us by the stars,
Let's feel a flight and a torment, and a covenant for life.

An endless love embraces me when next to you,
Secretly I ask the sky to agree,
The free wind kisses our foreheads, with alabaster,
And holding hands, under the vaults, we whisper hidden thoughts.

An endless love without tears and regrets ...

July 28, 2020

The Sunset in Your Eyes

You know what I like the most? The sunset in your eyes, when we
feel the night coming,
The horizon with the name of a single tower, in the distance,
When we decipher the world, the wonders,
Unanswered questions, the game of banality and love.

You know what I like the most? The sky's flames in your hair,
Radiating from the mirrors of your room,
That's where our story begins,
The story of everyone who feels, like us, the lost freedom.

And you know what I like the most?
The thought of flying soon, blue-winged birds,
Over the world full of tears, reborn,
The story of a new beginning, the sunrise in your infinite eyes.

January 31, 2021

74

http://bit.ly/ClaudiaManta